BMW

PRECISION AND PERFORMANCE

Paul W. Cockerham

PHOTOGRAPHY BY KLAUS SCHNITZER

SMITHMARK

This edition published in 1997 by
SMITHMARK Publishers, a division of U.S. Media Holdings, Inc.,
115 West 18th Street, New York, NY 10011

SMITHMARK books are available for bulk purchase for sales promotion and premium use.
For details write or call the manager of special sales,
SMITHMARK Publishers, 115 West 18th Street, New York, NY 10011

This book was designed and produced by
Todtri Productions Limited
P.O. Box 572, New York, NY 10116-0572
FAX: (212) 279-1241

Printed and bound in Singapore

Library of Congress Catalog Card Number 97-066048

ISBN 0-7651-9228-4

Author: Paul W. Cockerham

Publisher: Robert M. Tod
Editorial Director: Elizabeth Loonan
Book Designer: Mark Weinberg
Senior Editor: Cynthia Sternau
Project Editor: Ann Kirby
Photo Editor: Edward Douglas
Picture Researchers: Meiers Tambeau, Laura Wyss
Production Coordinator: Jay Weiser
Desktop Associate: Paul Kachur
Typesetting: Command-O design

Contents

Introduction

The Bavarian Motor Works (or Bayerische Motoren Werke, in the native German) was created on March 7, 1916, as an aircraft-engine manufacturing concern. Most of the engines made by the company were the design of Dr. Max Friz, a talented design engineer who had previously been employed by Mercedes.

The company's first significantly successful aircraft engine was the Type IIIa, an inline 6-cylinder unit that generated 185 horsepower. The engine was primarily used in Fokker D7s flown by such notable early aces as Ernst Udet and Manfred, Baron von Richthofen—the "Red Baron." It could power a biplane to 5,000 meters in altitude in just twenty-nine minutes—in 1918, a record.

BMW Hits the Ground Running

Under the Versailles treaty, the company was prohibited after World War I from manufacturing aircraft and aircraft engines, so BMW started looking for other engine-making opportunities. Max Friz wanted BMW to get into the motorcycle business, so he designed a prototype that used a 500-cubic-centimeter engine of twin opposing cylinders (called a "boxer" after the cross-punching appearance of the horizontal pistons and connecting rods); it drove the rear wheel through a driveshaft and was mounted on a double-tube frame. Production of the R32 motorcycle started in 1923, and to this day, its basic technology—shaft drive, boxer engine—is a hallmark of the company's motorcycles.

Management had repeatedly discussed getting into the automobile business, and finally did so in late 1928 when BMW acquired the Eisenach Vehicle Factory (named after the city it was founded in), located 200 miles north of Munich. The company had already been making cars for twenty-nine years, and at the time of purchase was engaged in making a single model, a licensed version of the British Austin Seven. This was BMW's first automobile, known as the 3/15 or Dixi; BMW put their badge on it in April 1929.

A 24-valve 3.5-liter inline six powers this mighty M6. The forward-thrusting snout proudly proclaims that this car takes no prisoners.

It wasn't until 1932 that BMW was finally able to put its own mark on a vehicle, when it produced a new, larger version of the Dixi known as the 3/20. But cars were still a minor part of the company's production, which was again largely devoted to airplane engines (the Versailles manufacturing restrictions were lifted in 1922).

A Reputation is Built

BMW's reputation as a manufacturer of sports sedans arose when the 6-cylinder 303 was introduced in 1933. The following year, its engine was enlarged from 1.2 to 1.5 liters; it was then called the 315. A sports roadster, the 315/1, soon followed.

Despite the Depression and the political turmoil of the '30s, the period marked the ascendancy of BMW as a recognized manufacturer of high-quality sporting vehicles. Such cars as the compact 326 sedan, the sophisticated 327 coupe and convertible, and the pulse-quickening 328 roadster were much sought after by automobile cognoscenti.

The company was starting to make a reputation on the track as well, achieving considerable success in their racing efforts. A streamlined version of the 328 won Italy's famed Mille Miglia in 1940. But war production put BMW temporarily out of the automobile business soon afterward.

All BMW cars to this point had been built in Eisenach, located in what was now, as of 1945, East Germany. The bombed-out Munich plant in the west was rebuilt, and motorcycle production was resumed.

FOLLOWING PAGE: The "L" in the 3.0 CSL's nomenclature stood for "light-weight"; this signi-fied the car's use of an aluminum hood, doors, and trunk lid, which al-lowed a total weight of only 2,794 lbs.

This family portrait of "M" series perfor-mance cars, features, in front, an example of the mid-engined M1 coupe.

This Veritas-BMW Rennsport spyder, unpainted, nicely shows off the undu-lating lines of its aluminum coachwork.

Pictured here on the grounds of the U.S. Air Force Academy in Colorado are a 3200 CS coupe and a red 503 coupe. Both were powered by iterations of BMW's first post-war V-8 engine.

One of the company's first post-war automotive efforts was a tiny, bubble-shaped vehicle powered by a motorcycle engine. Known as the Isetta, the car was eagerly embraced by a cash-strapped public still dealing with petroleum shortages.

But it wasn't too long before BMW was back producing elegant, high-performance vehicles. A sedan model known as the 501 first appeared in 1952; it was soon followed by the 502 series, which was powered by Germany's first post-war V-8 engine to see production. The 502 had a couple of dashing relatives—the 503 coupe and cabriolet. A particularly exquisite roadster, the 507 debuted in 1957, and to this day remains a highly desirable collectible.

Performance and Style

The company's contemporary age began with the introduction of the 1500 sedan in 1962. It was a thoroughly modern family sedan with an overhead-cam, 4-cylinder engine, front disc brakes, and independent suspension on all four wheels. Its styling was not too flashy, but since Germans did not have a speed limit impeding their progress on the highways, the car did have high-performance driving dynamics.

A two-door version soon followed, which ultimately led to a family of cars that introduced many Americans to the sports-sedan concept: the 2002 series. The company soon launched a new generation of 6-cylinder cars as well; these included the Bavaria sedan and the 3.0 CS coupe.

The model line that represents the company today first started to take shape with the debut of the 5 series in 1972. Over the past two decades, continuous iterations of these vehicles, as well as 5, 6, 7, and 8-series cars, have helped enhance the company's reputation for clean design, quality engineering, ergonomics, and lively performance.

This reputation struck a chord with a rising generation of young American professionals during the 1980s, and the marque quickly became a status symbol. Having a "Beemer" meant that you had arrived, and had an appreciation for the performance and engineering elegance found in these cars.

Champion Racing Cars

Such a solid package also became, in many instances, the foundation for championship production-based racing cars. BMW's engines powered the Brabham Formula One grand-prix car that Nelson Piquet drove to the world championship in 1983.

During the 1970s, a series of racing machines—"art cars"—was hand-painted by such modern masters as Alexander Calder, Frank Stella, and Andy Warhol. After being raced in events such as the 24 hours of LeMans, these cars were fittingly displayed in the BMW Museum in Munich and continue to be displayed at art galleries and car events around the world.

Multinational

Today, BMW is a global enterprise, with thirteen subsidiaries in Germany as well as twenty-seven foreign subsidiaries. BMW recently opened a state-of-the-art facility in South Carolina which builds their Z3 two-seat roadsters. There is a design studio in California, and a new Research and Engineering Center in Munich, advanced in both operating concept and in the futuristic nature of its products, creating what will no doubt be standard-bearers for performance and sophistication in the next millennium. As these pages will attest, BMW has been striving toward this goal throughout its history.

The "M" cars, known primarily as high performance automobiles, are no slouch in the appointments department either. The optional custom leather interior of this M5 features hides on the dashboard as well!

Buying the Eisenach facility brought
BMW the production rights to the
Dixi, a licensed version of the British
Austin Seven sedan that boasted 15 h.p.

Chapter One

From the Beginning Through the 2002

The Bavarian Motor Works, largely through the initiative of Dr. Max Friz, a brilliant design engineer who made his reputation at Mercedes prior to World War I, had made several early forays into automobile production prior to buying the Eisenach Automobile Factory in October of 1928. There had been a sports prototype called the Sascha, designed by Dr. Ferdinand Porsche, and there was an aerodynamic front-wheel-drive car, of which three prototypes, wearing an SHW badge, were made.

Humble Dixi Roots

Buying the Eisenach facility brought with it production rights to the Dixi, a licensed version of the British Austin Seven sedan. This was not a particularly auspicious beginning for a company that would go on to be known as a master manufacturer of performance sedans and coupes. The Dixi 3/15 had a small, side-valve, 4-cylinder, 749-cubic-centimeter engine that developed, at best, 15 horsepower. Its top speed was all of 53 miles per hour. But it represented a sound, basic concept that also took root in other parts of the world; Austin licensed production of the Seven in the United States, Belgium, France, and even Japan. There were plenty of buyers, particularly after the Wall Street crash of 1929.

As for the Dixi, BMW used some rather imaginative sales methods, including hire/purchase agreements. When BMW ended its agreement with Austin in 1932, 15,948 Dixi 3/15s had been built.

By this time, BMW had on the drawing board its own, enlarged version of the Dixi, a car with an overhead-valve engine that was larger (782 cubic centimeters) and more powerful (20 horsepower). Built from 1932 to 1934, the AM (for "Auto München," even though the car was built in Eisenach) 3/20 reached sales levels in excess of 7,000. It was also a popular platform for several European coach-builders, including Mercedes, which produced a variety of open and closed 3/20s.

Inline 6-cylinder engines, a focus of BMW production throughout the company's history, first appeared at the Berlin auto show in 1933 in the model 303. The 30-horsepower mill provided a foundation for subsequent generations of BMW engines, while the grille in front of it had a distinctive kidney shape to it that would be immortalized, with some variations, in every BMW automobile that followed it.

Pre-War Classics

From 1933 until 1939, when the war caused the suspension of automobile production, BMW produced a series of 4- and 6-cylinder automobiles that are regarded by many as classics.

The 328 caused a minor furor among sports car enthusiasts when it was introduced—they felt its springing was too soft for a performance car. Success on the race track soon won over skeptics.

Roughly half of the BMW collection of Dr. Gerhard Knöchlein, shown at an estate near Nuremburg, Germany: In the second row, far left, is one of only two 328 Wendling coupes known to exist. The collection is considered the premier grouping of BMWs in private hands.

Ernst Loof, a former BMW employee, created a stunning and sophisticated sports racer, the Veritas-BMW Rennsport spyder, in 1949, based on 328 mechanicals.

The first of these, the 309, introduced a system of badging logic that has more or less continued to this very day, as the "09" signified that the car had a 0.9-liter, 4-cylinder engine.

The 315 of 1934 was a sporting 6-cylinder car that emerged when the engine from the 303 was bored out to 1.5 liters. This engine, fitted with twin Solex carburetors, had a 5.6:1 compression ratio and was good for 34 horsepower.

A two-seater little brother soon followed, the 315/1. Its engine was fitted with triple carburetors and taller heads, providing 8:1 compression. Its 40 horsepower could propel the 315/1 to 75 miles per hour. BMW first tasted the fruits of racing success with this model in rally events. Bored-out versions of these cars—the 319 and 319/1—followed.

Unique details of the interior of the 327 convertible includes white-on-black instrumentation, an enameled steering rim, horn button and shift knob, and locks for the sectioned, foldable windscreen.

The Sleek 320s

The company truly established itself as a producer of quite beautiful automobiles with the 326, 327, and 328 cars. The badging protocol was temporarily abandoned during this period, as all three lines were powered by a 1,971-cubic-centimeter, 4-cylinder engine.

Of these, the 328 is the best known, even though only 462 were constructed. The lines of the car would influence BMW designs through the mid-'50s, and its performance dynamics were incredibly well balanced for the era. The chassis was made of tubular steel, strong and light in weight; the suspension, with a live rear axle and a transverse sprung-wishbone configuration in the front. As a two-seater, the 328 weighed a mere 1,826 pounds. The hemispherical-head 2-liter engine, with its triple Solex carburetors, had little trouble propelling the 328 to speeds that complemented its superb handling.

The 327 convertible, powered by a 1,971-cc 4-cylinder engine, showed the company's penchant for marrying sophistication and performance in its designs.

The mark of a nicely restored vintage car is an engine compartment that is clean and finely polished, but not so much that it eclipses the rest of the automobile. This 327 convertible shows a fine example of such detailing.

Triple Solex carburetors, each with its own air cleaner, helped the 328's 2.0-liter, hemispherical head engine to breath easily, giving the 1,826-lb. car lively performance.

The 328 is the best known of BMW's early cars, even though only 462 were constructed. The lines of the car would influence the company's designs through the mid-'50s.

German cars in general, and BMWs in particular, are known for clear, unclut-tered instrument panels, such as that found in this 1939 327/28 coupe.

Note the nicely proportioned rear wheel covers on the 327. An affinity for ele-gant design has always been a hallmark of cars produced by the Munich firm.

With sleek body-work by Graf Goertz, the 503 coupe, built between 1956 and 1959, had a 140-h.p. aluminum V-8 that stopped the German press from complaining about weak engines, but did nothing for the company's bottom line.

An Interruption

When World War II intervened, BMW concentrated solely on producing aircraft engines; the company achieved some notoriety for its pioneering efforts in the development of tur-bojet and rocket-engine power. Under post-war, Allied control, the company's factories were limited to making cookware, and motorcycle production did not resume until 1948.

Getting back into the car business would prove to be difficult. In the interim, the most significant developments were initiated independently by enthusiasts such as Ernst Loof, a former BMW employee who created a stunning and sophisticated sports racer, the Veritas-BMW Rennsport spyder, in 1949.

The company's first post-war vehicle was the 501 saloon, which debuted at the Berlin show in 1951. Critics felt that the four-door looked too much like the Austin Seven, and that the 1,971-cubic-centimeter 6-cylinder was too poky. Money was tight for BMW, which might explain the lack of creativity seen in the 501, as well as the fact that body construction was subcontracted to the Baur firm in Stuttgart. Still, nearly 5,700 units were sold between 1952 and 1955.

The company soon developed the first production V-8 engine seen in Germany since the war, a 90-degree bank unit of 2,580 cubic centimeters that produced 95 horsepower. The 502 saloon it powered first came on the scene as a production model in 1954. A coupe and cabriolet variant called the 503 had an engine tweaked to 140 horsepower, and a fabu-lously sophisticated two-seater, the 507 roadster, designed by Graf Goertz, was good for 150 horsepower.

Critics stopped complaining in the presence of these cars, but they did absolutely nothing for the company as a business proposition. What ultimately propelled BMW's automobile business into the black was a license agreement with the Italian manufacturer Iso to produce the tiny, two-seat Isetta "bubble car."

The unfortunate nickname of the Isetta came from its extraordinarily narrow rear track as well as its door—the front panel of the coachwork. Over the years they were powered with BMW motorcycle engines, and small ones at that: 245 and 298 cubic centimeters, which provided fuel economy of 53 miles per gallon.

But the Isettas were a hit with the road-going public, and ultimately more than 161,000 were manufactured and sold. Compare this with the sales achieved by the company's own designs: Total manufacturing for the big 6-cylinder 501 and V-8 502 lines only reached 23,120 vehicles by 1959. The 507 roadster saw only 253 examples built over three years. One special limited-run project was a state limousine made for the West German chancellor, Konrad Adenauer; two examples of the 505 limousine saw the light of day.

Manufactured under license from Iso, the BMW Isetta bubble car helped the company regain financial footing in the 1950s. More than 161,000 of the little cars were sold.

At these levels, the corporation survived only on its healthy business from motorcycles. As the 1950s drew to a close, BMW introduced the 600 line, based on a 2-cylinder boxer engine which was based on their renowned motorcycle engine. The 600s were notable in their use of a trailing-arm rear suspension, a refinement that ultimately became part of the company's basic approach to automobile design.

The 600's engine was ultimately enlarged. New sedan and coupe bodies, penned by Michelotti, were created, and thus a new model series, the 700, was born. The volume of sales created by the 700 line from 1959 through 1965 helped the company gain cash reserves that saved it from bankruptcy. More than 181,000 700s were purchased during this period; 40 horsepower and 40 miles per gallon were a reasonable combination of power and economy, and the car accelerated to 62 miles per hour 6 seconds faster than its primary competition, the British Austin Mini. The little air-cooled engine, slightly tweaked, also powered the 700 sport coupe model to several race and rally wins, and the company was on its way to building a racing legacy.

BMW's Trademark Style Emerges

The 700 was immensely popular with the growing West German middle class, and the cash reserves it produced for the company were reinvested in the model that would follow, a larger car that would enjoy even greater sales success worldwide. This car was the 1500. A practical four-door sedan, it was powered by a 1.5-liter, 4-cylinder engine, with a single overhead camshaft driven by a chain, an aluminum head with hemispherical combustion chambers, and a five-bearing steel crankshaft.

As the company was planning on enlarging this basic engine down the road (as it would do in 1.6-, 1.8-, and 2-liter variants), it was made to withstand tremendous loads. Production vehicles would ultimately produce 170 horsepower, but the same basic cast-iron block was used in turbocharged

The business office of a late-'50s vintage 507 roadster. Compare its elegantly simple detailing to the more vulgar excesses found in American cars of the period.

The lines of the 1956–59 507 are very much part of the jet age from whence it came. Only 253 of these hand-built beauties were created, and less than 75 examples remain.

This 700 Sport cabriolet dates from the early '60s. The vents on the deck lid signify the car's rear-engined configuration.

BMW bought the Glas company and produced a small number of automobiles in the '60s using leftover Glas bodies. Among these was the 1600 GT. This is the best angle from which to view the car.

grand-prix racing engines in the early 1980s, monsters that produced in excess of 1,200 horsepower.

This engine was installed in the 1500 in an upright position, but in its later, larger manifestations, the engine would be canted 30 degrees to the right, allowing the designers to use a low hood line that would come to be a BMW signature. The 1500 was also kitted out with worm-gear steering and independent suspension all around: MacPherson struts in the front, and an update of the company's trailing-arm design in the rear. Disc brakes were found in front, drums in the rear. Initial cars were produced in a rush to meet exhibit requirements for the fall 1961 Frankfurt motor show, and the quality of these first cars suffered for it, but most production bugs had been taken care of when full production began in October 1962.

It was a significant car for BMW, for it bore all of the basic characteristics that the company would thereafter market to its domestic middle-class customers. More than 23,000 1500s were made between 1962 and 1964.

But it was a slightly larger car, the 1800, that would prove more popular. Available as a four-door sedan in both base and 1800TI (for *tourismo internationale*) models of 90 or 110 horsepower, more than 92,000 1800s left the factory between 1963 and 1968. Of these, 567 were a special, competition-only model, the 1800TI/SA, which could tear along the autobahn at nearly 120 miles per hour as it went to and from the numerous races and rallies in which it competed.

Breaking New Ground: The "02"

The next growth was to a 2-liter car, the 2000, of which 140,000 examples were made between 1966 and 1972. But the car that really launched the company into the hearts of sports-driving enthusiasts was the "02" model, built from 1966 to 1976.

The designation originated from a car exhibited at the Geneva show of 1966, the 1600–2. The company had primarily built four-door autos for years, and it wanted to show it could produce a car with a smaller and lighter body.

By far the most famous car BMW ever built was the 2002. Americans went absolutely bonkers over the car, buying it for the sheer joy of driving it represented.

About as rare a BMW as you'll ever find is this 1974 1802 Touring, a three-door hatchback fitted with an early company 5-speed gearbox. Less than a thousand examples were produced that year.

The running componentry was standard BMW: MacPherson struts and discs in front, trailing arms and drums in back, and worm-gear steering. The transmission was a four-speed manual unit; soon a five-speed box would be an option.

By far the most famous car BMW ever built was the 2002. Americans went absolutely bonkers over the car, buying it for the sheer joy of driving it represented. The 02 cars had particularly narrow A, B, and C pillars framing vast expanses of glass; not only did they offer the driver superb visibility, but they also emphasized an aggressive shape below the cowl line. The 1,990-cubic-centimeter engine provided 100 horsepower and a 110-miles-per-hour top speed, as well as fuel economy better than 25 miles per gallon. The comfortable and well-balanced suspension allowed drivers to practice sliding the tail out under power whenever they wanted a little fun.

The car ultimately had a twin-carburetor variant, the 2002TI, which put out an additional 20 horsepower, as well as a fuel-injected version, the 2002tii, good for 130 horsepower. Smaller cars, the 1602 and 1802, were available for the European market; the 1602 was the best-selling model in the entire line on the Continent, with nearly 173,000 models built. The basic 2002 sold at a level of more than 152,600 units in Europe, as well as nearly 44,000 cars in the U.S., between 1968 and 1973.

Both the 1602 and 2002 were available in Europe as convertibles, thanks to coachwork made by Baur of Stuttgart. They had somewhat inferior driving characteristics compared to the hardtops, as the top provided a degree of structural rigidity.

The ultimate manifestation of the 02 series was the 2002 turbo. Turbocharging had helped the factory win a European touring-car championship in 1969, and the idea found its way into production prototypes by 1973, with full production starting the following year. The cars were aggressive looking, with both front and rear spoilers, but they were not warmly received by a public concerned with fuel shortages and costs in the wake of the Arab/Israeli conflict of 1973–74.

The company had made performance modifications to the chassis and brakes and installed a limited-slip differential, so the 2002 turbo provided a stunning driving experience. This 4-cylinder car could reach 131 miles per hour and accelerate to 60 miles per hour in less than 8 seconds

But politics and technology were catching up with the company, and it was time for a retooling. BMW had reached full maturity in producing the 2002, and the public had taken the car to heart. The modern era beckoned.

Generations of Bimmers: the 320 on the left was first introduced in 1975 to succeed the venerable four-cylinder 2002. More refined and safer than its predecessor, the 320 was nonetheless a heavier car, and initially lacked the 2002's performance. The 2002Tii on the right was good for 130 h.p.

*A comparative rarity is this 1987 325iX.
With four-wheel drive, a 5-speed manual transmission, and 168 h.p. on call,
a snowy road doesn't stand a chance.*

CHAPTER TWO

Contemporary Sedans

By the late 1960s, BMW was back on sound enough financial footing that its management thought it was time to take on rival maker Mercedes with a larger automobile. The company tackled the project in typical fashion, building on what it already knew.

Great Driving Machines

What it knew best was the 2-liter, 4-cylinder engine. Taking on Mercedes meant developing a new 6-cylinder mill, which BMW's engineers accomplished simply by adding two additional cylinders to the 4-banger. The new 2.5-liter inline 6 had a slightly smaller bore and stroke found in the smaller unit, was mounted at the same 30-degree slant, and produced 150 horsepower. Production of the new car, the 2500, began in August 1968; an additional model with stouter bore and stroke dimensions, the 2800, followed six months later.

Mechanically, the cars used running gear typical of what had been employed throughout the company's history: MacPherson struts in front, trailing-arm linkage in back (with Boge self-leveling shocks in the 2800). A three-speed automatic transmission was an option on the standard four-speed manual. The bigger 2800, with its 20 additional horsepower and 124-miles-per-hour top speed, mandated more substantial braking capacity, so it was fitted with disc brakes all around.

The cars did the company proud, and essentially opened up a new market for a prestige car that emphasized the driving experience over creature comforts. It would grow one more time into the 3.0S series, with the bore and stroke of the 6 now matching the 4-cylinder unit from which it came. Initially the cars had carbureted engines that produced 180 horsepower at 6,000 rpm, but in 1974 a fuel-injected variant, the 3.0Si, was offered, which produced 200 horsepower (European)at 5,700 rpm. For a big car, the 3.0Si was rapid, offering a top speed in excess of 130 miles per hour.

Long-wheelbase models were offered as well, cars that, as of 1974, had an even bigger 3.3-liter 6, which put out 195 horsepower in fuel-injected trim.

These larger cars, as well as the family-oriented 5 series cars that debuted in 1972, fueled the thinking behind the vehicles that ultimately replaced the 02 line. BMW recognized that customers wanted a car that was more refined, safer, and better ventilated, and in 1975 unveiled its first 3 series line, known internally at Munich as the E21.

The 3 Series is Born

These cars were initially powered by the 2-liter 4, so the first models were called the 320. The basic BMW running gear was reconfigured to bring handling up to contemporary standards, and the long-held worm-gear steering box was replaced by a rack-and-pinion unit. The 320, however, was not as spartan an accommodation as was the 2002, and as its engine was required to power more accessories and move more weight, as well as cope with evolving anti-pollution measures, its performance was not as sprightly as the 02s.

A study in basic chromatic minimalism featuring the hind-quarter view of an E30 series M3 coupe. At the speeds this car could reach, it could certainly make use of a spoiler to help keep its tail on the ground.

BMW, however, left enough room in the engine bay to accommodate its 6-cylinder engines, and these brought the performance of the small BMW up to traditional levels. The E21 3 series enjoyed a long and profitable run, with more than 1.36 million cars being produced between 1975 and 1982.

Subtle refinements were barely apparent in the next-generation 3 series, code-numbered the E30, but it proved to be even more solid a car than the E21. More than 2.2 million of these cars were sold during its eleven-year run, in a staggering array of models. Sedans, convertibles, and even station wagons

This interior view of a contemporary M3 nicely shows the side and thigh bolsters of the upgraded seats, necessary given the high lateral g-force numbers the car's maneuverability can create.

Upgraded wheels have always been a feature of the M3, as is the case with this 1980s-vintage E30-series vehicle.

The rear of the 323i Touring model provides basketsful of storage space.

This roof shot of the 323i Touring provides a glimpse into the car's duality: a sunroof for fun, and roof racks for utility.

This idyllic setting nicely illustrates the getaway capacity of BMW's 4-cylinder station wagon, the 323i Touring.

(the "Touring" model), in two- and four-door editions, could be had. Engines ranged from a 4-cylinder diesel (non-USA) unit that produced 98 horsepower (for those interested in the mileage and high reliability inherent in diesel-engined cars), to the fuel-injected, 2.58-liter 6, good for 168 horsepower.

Part of this family was powered by a new generation of small, 6-cylinder engines. A 2-liter 6 powered the 320i/6, as well as the larger 520i. The 323i got a larger 2.3-liter unit.

The 1985 325 four-door was a small family sedan with plenty of oomph. The reason? A nifty little 2.5-liter six-cylinder engine, good for 168 h.p.

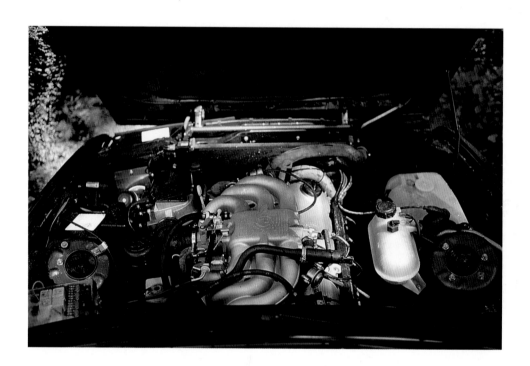

A 1985 325 sedan such is this is most representative of BMW's E30 series of automobiles, which, in several body styles, totaled more than 2.2 million units over an eleven-year production run.

Z for Zoom

This latter engine also powered an unusual pure sports car, the Z1. The little two-seater had a galvanized steel chassis and bolt-on plastic body panels. Even weight distribution was achieved by placing the engine behind the front axle line. The drivetrain was attached to a new central-arm, multiple-link rear suspension. On the road, the car would go where it was pointed, at up to 136 miles per hour A particularly noteworthy feature was drop-down side door panels that accentuated the open-air driving experience. The Z1 was built from 1988 to 1990, with eight thousand units leaving the Munich assembly line.

Introduced in 1996, the Z3 is a fabulous little two-seat roadster, a pure sports car that initially suffered from a reputation as being underpowered, given that it was offered with a 1.9-liter 4-cylinder mill. The public flocked to it, and it certainly didn't hurt that the car had a featured role in a contemporary James Bond film, *Goldeneye*. The power challenge was met late in 1996, when the Z3 2.8 (named for its 6-cylinder engine), debuted. With a more aggressive front spoiler and a wider rear track than its little brother, the Z3 2.8 made an already great-looking car appear more serious. The additional power (up to 189 horsepower from 138) allowed for further exploration of the potential of the chassis, providing throttle correction for oversteer and a generally more satisfying drive. A coupe version is slated to be offered at the end of 1998.

Just enough room for two to have fun: the cockpit of the Z3 roadster. The top retracts manually and stores beneath a soft cover.

The 316i compact (sold as the 318ti in the United States, thanks to a larger 4-cylinder engine) is a comparatively inexpensive hatchback, providing an "entry-level" BMW experience.

The 316i compact is powered by a 1.6-liter inline four and provides a reasonable balance between performance and economy.

Today's 3 Series

Contemporary BMW 3 series cars start with the 318ti. A bob-tailed, three-door hatchback powered by a 1.9-liter 4, the car was created specifically to provide relatively inexpensive entry into the BMW line. Aficionados consider it a worthy spiritual successor to the VW GTI—short and squat, it resembles a rally car, and the driver has to keep the engine revving high to get maximum performance out of it.

The current 3 series 6-cylinder offering, the 328i, is a fine all-around enthusiast's car, athletic and graceful. The clutch operates with easy slickness, and the gearshift moves through the gate with a satisfying smoothness. The car's steering is precise, through an engine-speed-sensitive, variable-assist mechanism. The chassis is responsive, and the driver has merely to step on the gas to kick out the rear end whenever desired.

The 328i's straight 6 pulls the car to speed in a linear fashion, no matter how many rpms show on the tachometer. It offers 190 horsepower, 206 pound-feet of torque, and 0-to-60 times in 7 seconds flat, while seating four in sophisticated comfort.

M3—A Connoisseur's Car

For many performance enthusiasts today, the ultimate car to buy is the BMW M3. The latest iteration in a long line of M3s has a 3,152-cubic-centimeter, dual-overhead-cam, 6-cylinder engine that puts out 321 horsepower in European

A distinguishing feature on the M3 Lightweight is the added lip found at the bottom of the front air dam.

These lovely alloy rims, and high-performance ultra-low-profile tires, are found on the M3 Lightweight.

The business office of the M3 Lightweight coupe. You won't find air-conditioning controls here—the unit was sacrificed to improve performance.

specs, 240 horsepower in American. Its sharp throttle response meets the road through a five-speed manual transmission in the two-door coupe; a five-speed automatic is available in the new M3 four-door sedan. The chassis has been described by enthusiast publications as being "outstanding." It features a switchable traction-control system along with upgraded steering, firmer suspension, and ultra high-performance brakes..

Even though it can grab corners in an uncanny manner and hold the road as though glued, the M3 also offers a very civilized ride. Passengers enjoy automatic climate control, a top-flight stereo system, and comfortable sport seats.

The M3 family, as available in Europe, includes a convertible as well as a four-door sedan and a two-door coupe.

The epitome of the small sporting automobile has to be BMW's M3 Lightweight, where refinements such as high performance brakes and aluminum doors helped make an already nimble car even lighter on its feet.

The contemporary E36-based M3 features a switchable traction control system along with upgraded steering, firmer suspension, and more powerful brakes.

FOLLOWING PAGE: The interior of the 528i, like that of every BMW, is designed to facilitate the driver's interaction with the car.

The 5 Series

The company's mid-sized 5 series cars offer the ultimate experience in driving a family sedan. They, too, have a noted history of performance, with some production models inspired by the Motorsport division.

One such car was the M535i of 1979–80. It had the 218-horsepower, 6-cylinder engine from the big 735i sedan; down the road the car evolved into a second-generation version badged the M5 in 1985.

What more could the successful executive family man want? With its 286-horsepower, 3.5-liter engine, the M5 was a four-door sedan that could fly along at 150 miles per hour The large 6-cylinder engine had grown to 3.8 liters by the 1990s, and could be found in both four-door sedan and M5 Touring (station wagon) model (unlike their American counterparts, Europeans like the idea of high-performance station wagons).

In its lineage, the M5 had perhaps the most unusual vehicle ever produced by the Munich firm. The madmen in Motorsport had managed to massage the big 6-cylinder engine into producing 470 horsepower for racing by the late 1970s; this outrageous performance was destined to be fitted into a two-seat, mid-engine road car, the M1. Capable of 160-miles-per-hour top speeds, the car was

The family-oriented 5 series cars have always been BMW's main competitive weapon against Mercedes. Shown here is a 525i from 1989.

In recent years the company's Motorsports division has tricked up production vehicles for public consumption; these receive the designation "M5."

The quin-
tessential
BMW—the
mid-sized
sedan, pow-
ered by an in-
line 6-cylinder
engine—ably
represented
by the 528i.

Motoring jour-
nalists around
the world have
pronounced
the 528i one
of the most
well-balanced
cars ever
manufactured.

What motor-
ing is all
about: a safe,
powerful car
(here, a 528i)
opening up
vistas of
breathtaking
beauty.

A station wagon—preferably in red—is standard operating equipment for many well-off rural residents. The 525 Touring brings performance to such issues of lifestyle.

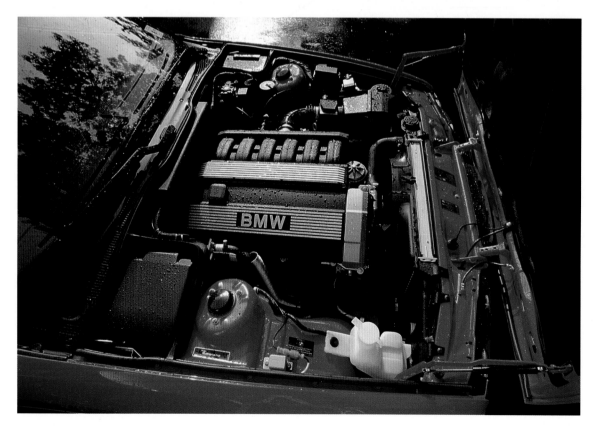

Buying a station wagon doesn't necessarily mean one needs to pay a price in performance—under the hood, the 525 Touring is all BMW.

also safe when taken to the limit of its capabilities. The M1 was the basis for a special one-marque racing series that was part of the undercard for Grand Prix racing during the 1980–81 series, called Procar. Racing legends Niki Lauda and Nelson Piquet, respectively, took the titles during the series' brief and expensive history.

Today, the 5 series is represented by the 528i, which has the same engine as the 328i and is a wonderfully balanced automobile. Somewhat heavier, and a tad nose-heavy by some lights, is the 540i, which is fitted with a 4,429-cubic-centimeter V-8 engine that packs quite a wallop. The European-spec car is limited by a computer chip to a top speed of 155 miles per hour; the American version only gets up to 128, which is governed by computer chip. In either case, the engine is strong and reliable. The American car has a five-speed ZF automatic transmission, or a six-speed manual that begs the driver to take the mid-sized Beemer to the limit, where it belongs.

As is the case with most European car manufacturers, BMW offers a greater choice of models to residents of the Continent than it does to American buyers, and this is certainly the case with the 5 series. Six sedan and four touring versions are available in Europe, including the 6-cylinder 520i, the 523i (actually powered by a 170-horsepower, 2.5-liter 6), the 525tds (a turbo-diesel), 528i, 535i, and 540i.

The 525i Touring is meant to appeal to BMW customers who'd like a bit of utility to go along with the car's elegance and performance.

The Ultimate in Luxury

At the top of the BMW sedan hierarchy is the 7 series, which, in contemporary times, is represented by the 750iL. The car is the most luxurious that BMW has ever created. It has an interior that has the ambiance, in the words of *Motor Trend* magazine, of a "high-tech library." The front seats, for example, are adjustable sixteen ways, and include a separate rake adjustment for the upper torso. Even the rear seats have multiple adjustment controls. The steering wheel is leather covered, like the seats, and, also like the seats, is heated for those frosty mornings. A cellular telephone and a 14-speaker, 440-watt stereo are standard features as well.

"Standard" is the operative word here. There are no factory options on the 750iL except a new on-board navigation system. It is equipped with every conceivable hedonistic fantasy a driver could want, except a butler.

At the heart of things is a 5.4-liter, 322-horsepower, single-overhead-cam V-12 engine. The 4,553-pound car has a ZF five-speed automatic transmission, and it can go from 0 to 60 miles per hour in a very respectable 6.4 seconds. The box has a manual mode if the driver wants to hold in a particular gear, and a "sport" mode should an aggressive shifting pattern be desired. The traction-control system can even be switched off, in case the driver wants to squeal the tires on takeoff.

BMW's mightiest powerplant is this 5.4-liter V-12, here found in a 750iL ("L" for long wheelbase).

BMW's 7 series sedans offer every conceivable personal amenity a driver could reasonably want, except perhaps for a butler.

The mantle of BMW's large executive cruiser has been worn for years by the company's 7 series line of cars. Despite their relative size, their responsiveness compares favorably with smaller cars.

Yet the 750's 12-cylinder engine has been accused by some enthusiasts of not having enough torque at the low end. BMW remedied this in the early '90s by offering a 4-liter, 8-cylinder engine in the 7 series, a car that ultimately manifested itself as the 740iL. The 4-liter mill offered more accessible torque at higher revs, paradoxically creating a zippier driving experience for nearly $20,000 less than its 12-cylinder sibling.

Future Sedans

At this writing, BMW's newest sedans are starting to hit the market. The 540i is set to get a larger engine of 4.5 liters' displacement, although its badge will not change (this upgrade is being planned for the 740i and 740iL as well). The upgrade is designed to provide more mid-range and bottom-end torque, reducing inner friction, improving fuel economy, and reducing emissions.

The new 5 series Touring, which debuted in Europe in 1997, offers more room for back-seat passengers and luggage, more air bags, ride leveling and height adjustment capabilities, and the turbo-diesel engine as an option. The previous Touring's dual sunroofs and optional four-wheel drive have been eliminated.

Finally, set to debut sometime in the first half of 1998, is the long-overdue replacement for the high-performance M5 sedan. Lightweight suspension components and body panels will be featured, along with a six-speed manual sequential transmission and a more powerful 4.7-liter V-8. The engine will have adjustable intake and exhaust cams and should be good for about 375 horsepower, according to company insiders.

The 540i can reach a governed speed of 155 m.p.h. in European specs, thanks to its 4.4-liter V-8 engine and a 6-speed manual shifter.

The broad power band provided by the 740i's V-8 engine make the car, to many, preferable to the V-12 version, the 750i.

The placement of the company badge on the "C" pillar of this 3.0 CS, as well as the stylistic treatment it received, was unusual.

CHAPTER THREE

Of Coupes, Engineering, and Enthusiasts

The Munich company has traditionally produced a series of coupes that were more angular of line than its comparatively mainstream offerings, and powered by the strongest of BMW's engines. One example, the 3200CS, one of the more striking BMWs ever built, was in production from 1962 to 1965. Its body was shaped by the Bertone studio in Turin, Italy, and it was powered by the 3.2-liter, aluminum-alloy V-8, which provided 160 horsepower.

Racing Form

During the late '60s and early '70s, it was the 6-cylinder 3.0CS and CSi that carried the coupe mantle. The fuel-injected CSi's engine was good for 200 horsepower; one example carried Jeremy Walton and Peter Hanson to a first in class and seventh overall in the 1972 Spa-Francorchamps 24-hour race.

A black 3.0 CS coupe is shown with a true "mighty mite": a 2002 Turbo— the quickest 4-cylinder BMW made up to that time. It could reach 131 m.p.h.

FOLLOWING PAGE: The discerning eye will see the flares around the rear wheels that identify this Z3 as the 6-cylinder 2.8 model.

Had Klaus Schnitzer found a driver for this Alpina CSL, and were the car in motion on Laguna Seca's road course, would he have been able to capture the smile that would inevitably be on the driver's face?

A 3.2-liter V-8 powered the 3200 CS coupes built from 1962 through 1965. The alloy engine was good for 160 h.p.

This cabal of coupes shows BMW's evolving design philosophy. From the front, a 2000CS, a 3.0 CS, a 630, and a contemporary 12-cylinder 850.

This car was ultimately refined into the CSL (the "L" is for "lightweight") model. It was so named for the body, constructed with unstressed alloy panels, and its lighter weight made for livelier performance. As a competitive auto, the CSL was most successful in the European Touring Car Championship between 1973 and 1980, and also met with racing success in the American IMSA series.

The car was built in a variety of ways, some with triple-carbureted engines, some with Bosch D–Jetronic fuel injection. Cars sold in Germany were equipped with an optional aerodynamic spoiler kit; early cars sold in Great Britain were delivered without the spoilers, but with more luxurious amenities.

The company's desire to race soon dictated engine size in the CS coupes; displacement was ultimately raised to 3,153 cubic centimeters. This produced an engine good for 206 horsepower and 140 miles per hour.

The power compartment of this 3.0 CS contains an engine of 2,985 ccs, rated at 170 h.p. at 5,800 r.p.m. This engine in turn was the basis for a 3.5-liter racing program.

The clean elegance of a leather interior and a pillarless roofline contribute to the singular appeal of BMW's coupes, as with this 3.0 CS.

The low hoodline found on all BMWs received particular emphasis on the company's coupes. William Hofmeister created this rakishly elegant design.

BMW's 3.0 CSL coupe dominated the European Touring Car Championship from 1973–80. This shot nicely shows the Bosch D-Jetronic fuel injection system that gave the engine its oomph.

Casually known as the "Batmobile," the 3.0 CSL was shipped to German customers with its distinctive wing kit stowed in the trunk.

Although this shot was taken in the American Rockies, the landscape provides a fitting backdrop, given the 3.0 CSL's Bavarian heritage.

The 6 Series

The CS was replaced by the 6 series coupe in 1976, a car that enjoyed a four-teen-year production run. The car's lines were quite angular; to the author's eyes they resembled a wheeled shark more than anything else. It, too, ran successfully in the European Touring Car Championship, taking the title in 1986.

Based on the floor plan of the 5 series sedan to save weight, the car, known initially as the 630 CS, and eventually as the 635 CSi engine grew, helped maintain the sporting image of the larger 7 series cars. It could accelerate to 140 miles per hour, but did so at a slower pace than its predecessor.

The reason was weight. The new 6 series was more than 260 pounds heavier than the CS, while having only 18 more horsepower (218) to move it around. In the U.S., emissions restrictions dragged the output down to 176 horsepower.

BMW Motorsport GmbH leaves a distinctive imprint on the valve cover of this M6 engine.

A triumvirate of Bavarian muscle from 1989: an M5 sedan on the left, and a pair of M6 coupes—all cool, quick, and elegant.

Whether under its own power or on top of a carrier, the 630's swoopy lines give it a look that resembles nothing so much as a shark.

The 6 series' fastest manifestation was the M635CSi. It had what was actually a 3.4-liter engine, at least from June 1982 on, with four valves per cylinder. It hummed like a turbine up to 7,000 rpm and was good for 285 horsepower and 150 miles per hour. Its tuned rear suspension gave it uncanny manageability on the road, and it had flared wheel arches to give it a look befitting the hottest production car BMW made at the time.

By the late '80s, BMW's top-end performance cars wore badges that simply designated their sporting intent ("M") and the series; thus the M635 CSi became simply the M6, before the company introduced its most aggressive coupe design to date, the 8 series.

The spare elegance of the M6's business office is straightforward and uncluttered, cosseting the driver in high comfort yet letting him/her concentrate on the business at hand.

At the heart of the M6 is a powerplant that absolutely dominated European production car racing for an astonishing fourteen-year run, from 1976 to 1990.

It wouldn't have hurt to have had considerable success on the trading floor of the stock exchange if you wanted to buy a BMW M6.

Loaded

The 850Ci is the swoopiest-looking four-seater ever created by the company from Munich, but in its original form, its 5-liter V-12, while technically brilliant, did not provide performance that lived up to the car's look. Late in 1994, the Motorsport division finished a series of upgrades to the car that led to the introduction of the 850CSi.

The engine, now bored and stroked to 5.6 liters, and benefitting from lighter pistons, a higher compression ratio, and a low-resistance stainless-steel exhaust, saw horsepower bumped from 296 to 372. The car has the potential to go quite far beyond its electronically governed 155 miles per hour top speed. Zero-to-60 takes but 5.8 seconds, reached just in second gear of the six-speed manual transmission. The suspension was retuned and the ride height lowered, creating a car that sticks to the pavement as if it were Velcro. With the $3,000 gas-guzzler tax, American citizens pay approximately $102,000 for the privilege of owning what might very well be the ultimate BMW.

Critics felt that the original 850 didn't quite offer performance to go with its stunning looks; the 850CSi, with a 5.6-liter, 372-h.p. engine, took care of those complaints.

The original Z3 roadster was the most anticipated new BMW in several decades; a featured role in the James Bond film Gold- eneye *helped stir interest.*

Contemporary BMW enthusiasts who feel that the lines of the company's cars run a tad boxy would feel appeased by the sight of the 850 coupe.

The quintessential yuppie weekend car would have to be this 1986 3 series convertible, birthed just prior to the Oct. '87 Wall Street crash.

The 850 coupe is powered by a 5.0-liter V-12 engine rated at 296 h.p. The car's pop-up headlights are readily apparent in this shot.

Efficiency and Performance, Defined

What lies at the heart of each BMW assembled today are matters purely of efficiency and performance. Here follows a glossary of several technical features found in each BMW—features that give the car its essential character—starting with the chassis.

Alloy wheels. Wheels made of alloy are lighter than their steel counterparts, and because they are cast rather than bent and extruded, they look better as well. Strong, weight-efficient, and tastefully styled, the company currently offers alloy wheels on all its U.S. models. BMW wheels tend to run rather large in order to provide plenty of ventilation area for the brakes, and to allow for a wide tire footprint for cornering, dry traction, and braking.

All-season traction. BMW, like other automakers, offers a traction-control system, governed by computer. It modulates engine power and the rear brakes to reduce wheelspin during periods of low traction, thus enhancing the driver's control of the automobile. Each wheel has a speed sensor, which in turn provides input for the engine's electronic controls, reducing torque when wheelspin threatens, or increasing it if engine braking, under deceleration, should reduce traction. The sensors also provide input for the rear brakes, if needed. All-season traction is standard for all BMWs sold in the United States.

Camber. Camber is a measurement of the front wheels when they lean slightly out from the vertical plane. It is deliberately induced when a car steers as a means of contributing to directional stability. BMWs have a relatively large degree of camber.

Disc brakes. BMWs come with large disc-brake rotors. They are ventilated in front to enhance fade resistance on all BMWs save for 4-cylinder cars; the 328i convertible, M3, and 5 series, 7 series, and 8 series cars have ventilated rotors all around. All BMWs have been equipped with a four-wheel antilock braking system since 1986.

Positive steering offset. The front wheels of BMWs are offset so that a line drawn through the steering axis intersects the ground ahead of the car, inboard of a wheel's

Sculpted design of these forged alloy wheels, found on an 850 CSi, is not only beautiful, but functional—they aid in brake cooling.

The fluid lines of the E36-based 325 convertible-make the car one of the more attractive soft-top offerings on the market.

Nothing stimulates the spirit quite like a fast car that lets the world in. A lot of glass, a sunroof, and no door pillars illustrate how accommodating this 850CSi is in this regard.

centerline. The reason is that if a front tire blows out, the car's natural tendency to pull to the outside is countered.

Rear-wheel drive. Modern automobiles, particularly smaller and mid-sized cars, have front-wheel drive, which can provide more interior room and improved traction in bad driving conditions. BMW has kept its cars rear-wheel drive machines, believing that its customers prefer the handling characteristics. Such an arrangement optimizes weight distribution, and contributes to BMWs having handling characteristics more in line with that of a sports car than that of a traditional family sedan.

Subframe construction. The front and rear suspensions of BMWs are mounted on separate subframes, which helps reduce vibration and road noise, thanks to the use of tuned-rubber mounting bushings.

FOLLOWING PAGE: This Alpina CSL shows off the wonderful finish of its drivetrain and suspension components.

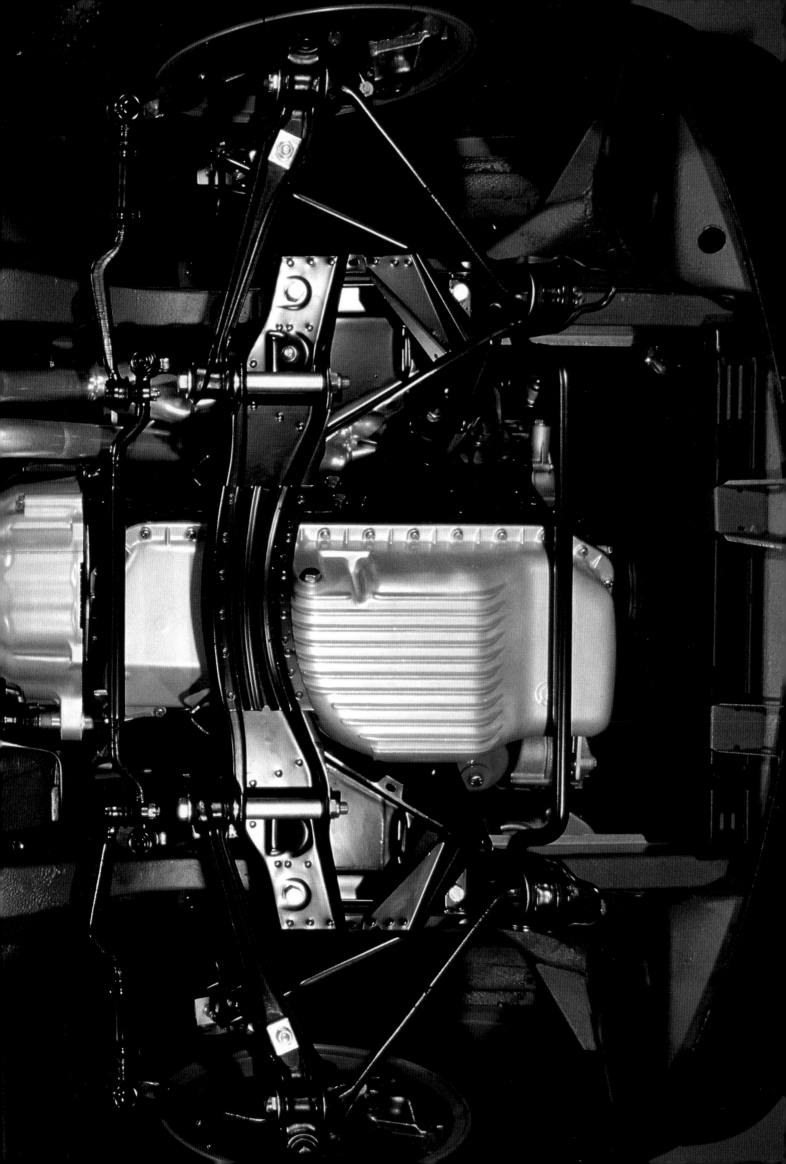

This 1987 325 convertible lets it all air out. The hardtop variants, though a sound design, required a number of major modifications to maintain the torsional rigidity of the convertible.

We now turn to performance and efficiency features found in the engine.

Chain camshaft drive. Many automobiles have camshafts driven by a toothed belt, which needs occasional inspection to check for wear. BMW engines currently have camshafts driven by chains, which are automatically kept at proper tension and are meant to last the lifetime of the car. The camshaft itself drives a valve mechanism that is adjusted by hydraulics automatically, creating a valvetrain that BMW claims requires no regular maintenance.

Crossflow aluminum cylinder heads. In a crossflow system, the engine's intake and exhaust systems lie on either side of the cylinder head, a configuration that encourages efficient airflow. Engine "breathing" and performance are thus improved. The heads' aluminum construction helps reduce weight and dissipate heat; dissipated heat allows for higher compression ratios, which also enhances performance. Aluminum is also used for the engine blocks of BMW's V-12s, V-8s, and the Z3 2.8 6-cylinder.

Direct ignition system. Each cylinder has its own ignition coil, instead of the conventional single coil for the entire engine. This keeps the number of moving parts down while suppressing electrical noise that can interfere with radio and telephone reception. It also generates a stronger spark in the compression chamber, while allowing for precise control of ignition timing in each individual cylinder.

Hydraulic engine mounts. All BMWs have hydraulic engine mounts, which employ oil as well as rubber to reduce engine vibration that could be felt inside the car.

Hydraulic valve adjustment. This system helps maintain zero clearance between the valves and their actuating mechanisms, minimizing valve noise and making periodic adjustment unnecessary. BMW's 6- and 8-cylinder engines have bucket-type hydraulic lifters between the camshaft's lobes and the valves; for the 4- and 12-cylinder engines, stationary adjusters position the pivots of the valve-actuating rocker arms.

Features such as those above have contributed to BMW's reputation as a well-engineered car, a trait that has become widely recognized by enthusiasts. This reputation has become as important a part of the BMW tradition as has the cars' renowned performance characteristics, adding to the uniqueness of Beemers in the minds of owners and enthusiasts.

With a new 2.8-liter 6-cylinder engine giving it added pep, the two-seat Z3 2.8 roadster provides tons of driving fun.

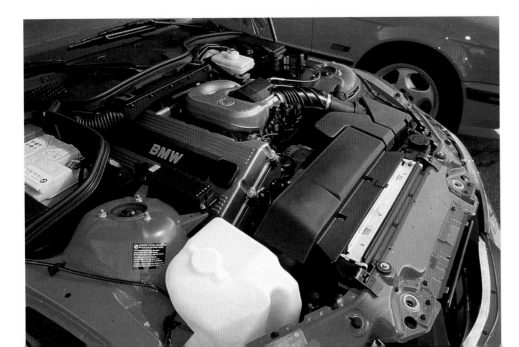

Although the engine compartment of the Z3 roadster appears snug, it is commodious enough to accommodate a longer 6-cylinder engine block. A 4-cylinder engine is shown here.

Pop master Andy Warhol painted this sleek M1, which finished sixth overall and second in class at LeMans in 1979. Just behind it is a Frank Stella 3.0 CSL from 1976.

Celebrations of the Marque

BMW fans like to celebrate this uniqueness. Consider the fact that BMW served as "featured marque" of the Monterey Historic Automobile Races in August 1996. The Monterey Historics annually attract automobile enthusiasts and collectors from around the world, and feature a series of historic car races arranged by class and vintage.

BMW presented some of its most famous racing machines, including a pre-war 328 that participated in the Mille Miglia (the 1,000-mile Italian road race), and a Brabham-BMW BT54 Formula One race car, similar to the BT52 that Nelson Piquet drove to the world championship in 1983.

"The Monterey Historic Automobile Races is the largest and most prestigious event in the world for connoisseurs of racing and vintage automobiles," commented Victor Doolan, president of BMW's U.S. sales and marketing subsidiary. "It is a high honor for BMW to be chosen as featured marque of the Monterey Historics, an honor shared with the greatest marques of the automobile world."

A colorful feature of the company's participation was the fact that it brought over the first four BMW "art cars," all of which participated in the 24 Hours of LeMans. They included the Alexander Calder 3.0 CSL from the 1975 race, a Frank Stella 3.0 CSL from 1976, the Roy Lichtenstein 320i that finished first in class and ninth overall in 1977, and the sleek Andy Warhol M1 that finished sixth overall and second in class in 1979.

A range of other BMW racing machinery was on display. Open-wheel machinery included a 1969 Dornier-BMW Formula Two car, the championship-winning 1979 March-BMW Formula Two machine, and the turbocharged 1986 Benneton-BMW Formula One car (the manufacturer of casual wear also makes and runs Formula One cars). Many production-based racers were present as well, including 3.0 CSL coupes campaigned in Europe in the early '70s, a Group 5 3.5 CSL from 1975, and a Group 5 M1 from 1980. Recent racers were on the scene as well, including a 1992 Group A M3 and a 1996 BMW-powered McLaren F1 GTR that had run at LeMans.

Cars that had run in American IMSA races were also on the scene, including several 3.5 CSLs, the 1978–79 320i turbos driven by David Hobbs and Jim Busby, several 1980 Group 4 M1s, and the 1982 BMW-March GTP car of Dave Cowart and Kenper Miller.

Some of BMW's most well known and successful drivers were also in attendance—names such as Nelson Piquet; Formula Two champion Marc Surer; BMW veteran Dieter Quester; IMSA GTO champions Cowart and Miller; Jim Busby; 3.0 CSL drivers Sam Posey and Brian Redman; IMSA champion and 2002/320i racer Nick Craw; current M3 driver Pete Halsmer; and the legendary Stirling Moss, who was taking hot laps in an old Frazer-Nash BMW, similar to one that belonged to his father that he drove early in his career.

It was a fine gathering, with representatives from the factory working with owners'-club officials to ensure that everybody had a good time. A BMW Car

Given Alexander Calder's penchant for designing sculpture and mobiles that appear to fly, his painting of this 3.0 CSL that ran at LeMans in 1975 seems a natural extension of his talents.

Club of America "corral" allowed everybody to show off what they brought, and parade laps were held on the famed Laguna Seca road course during the lunch break.

Watching the scene, Doolan observed, "BMW owners are just the most enthusiastic car owners in the world."

They have reason to be, and they enjoy celebrating their enthusiasm every chance they get. The BMW Car Club of America has an annual five-day celebration of the marque, called the Oktoberfest, which, paradoxically enough, is usually scheduled in summer. In 1997 it was held during the final week of July in Waterville Valley, New Hampshire.

A full range of enthusiast entertainment took place. Two car raffles were held; drivers' schools and advanced driving skills programs were held at New Hampshire International Speedway; an autocross and gymkhana ("fun" rally events) gave owners a chance to beat the clock; a *concours d'elegance* provided an opportunity to show the cars off in all their sparkling beauty; contests for trivia, model cars, and photos took place; and a full round of social events—receptions, cocktail hours, a clambake, and a belated Fourth of July celebration—provided a chance for friends new and old to talk about their favorite automobile.

Thus have BMW's engineers and enthusiasts conspired to celebrate their cars as exemplars of performance and efficiency. The company describes its vehicles as being "The Ultimate Driving Machine," yet BMW's products are considerably more down to earth than those available from supercar manufacturers such as Ferrari and Lamborghini. What makes the BMW unique is that it is indeed the ultimate in providing a driving experience tailored to the real world.

An overview of the 1996 BMW Car Club of America's annual "corral.

An M1 Procar and an Alpina CSL are seen at the 1996 Monterey Historic Automobile Races.

A collection of BMW "art" cars gather at the 1996 Monterey Historics. In front is the 320i, painted by Roy Lichtenstein, that finished first in class and ninth overall at the 24 Hours of LeMans in 1977.